Geography of
SOUTH AMERICA

by Kristine Hirschmann

Table of Contents

Pictures To Think About

GUYANA
Georgetown
SURINAME
Paramaribo
Cayenne
French Guiana
(FRANCE)

*ATLANTIC
OCEAN*

Manaus

BRAZIL

Brasília

PARAGUAY

Paraguay R.

São Paulo

Rio de Janeiro

Asunción

URUGUAY
Montevideo
Buenos Aires

ARGENTINA

N
W E
S

**Falkland Islands
(Islas Malvinas)
(U.K.)**

Words To Think About

Characteristics

- has many people
- has many buildings
- ?

urban

What do you think the word **urban** means?

Urban Places

- New York City
- Los Angeles
- ?

export

What do you think the word **export** means?

Latin:
ex
(out)

Latin:
portare
(to carry)

Read for More Clues

export, page 24
plain, page 3
urban, page 19

plain

What do you think the word **plain** means in this book?

Meaning 1
easy to understand
(adjective)

Meaning 2
simple; not fancy
(adjective)

Meaning 3
large, flat, grassy area
(noun)

Introduction

South America is one of Earth's seven **continents** (KAHN-tih-nents). It is easy to find this land mass on a map. But to really see it, you need to look at its **geography** (jee-AH-gruh-fee). Geography is the study of land and climate. These features affect where and how people live.

In this book, you will learn about South America. You will visit the tropical north. You will see the very cold south. You will also see some of the wettest and driest places on Earth.

▲ The Amazon River is the second-longest river in the world. It is home to more kinds of fish—about 2,500—than are found in the entire Atlantic Ocean.

South America has many regions. Each region has its own landscape. Some places have high mountain peaks. Others have flat, grassy **plains** (PLANEZ) and rivers.

Long ago, geography shaped where and how people lived. Today, those patterns of **settlement** (SEH-tul-ment) still affect countries, cities, cultures, and **trade**.

Read on. See how the landscape has shaped this continent's people and history.

Angel Falls in Venezuela is the ▲ highest waterfall in the world.

Physical Geography of South America

South America is the fourth-largest continent. It stretches about 4,700 miles (7,560 kilometers) from north to south.

South America is very wide in the north. It narrows to a point in the south. Its land area is about 6,880,000 square miles (17,819,000 square kilometers).

Part of the land lies north of the **equator** (ih-KWAY-ter). The equator is an invisible line. It divides Earth into northern and southern parts. Most of the continent lies south of the equator.

Seen from space, ▶
South America
looks a bit
like a huge
ice cream cone.

Location

South America is just below North America. A narrow strip of land joins the two land masses.

South America touches many different bodies of water. The Atlantic Ocean is to the east. The Pacific Ocean is to the west. The Caribbean (kair-ih-BEE-un) Sea is to the north. A cold stretch of water called the Drake Passage lies to the south. This passage is just 600 miles (966 kilometers) wide. On the other side is the frozen continent Antarctica.

❶ Solve This

It is about 800 miles (1,287 kilometers) from the top of South America to the equator. What percent of the continent's length lies south of the equator?

MATH ☑ POINT

What fact do you need to know about South America to solve this problem?

The Andes

The Andes (AN-deez) Mountains run down the west coast. The Andes are the longest mountain range on Earth. Many peaks are higher than 20,000 feet (6,096 meters). The tallest peak is Mount Aconcagua (ah-kone-KAH-gwah). This peak is 22,834 feet (6,960 meters) high.

The Andes range formed when two of Earth's plates collided. The plates pushed the land upward. This process also created volcanoes. The Andes have hundreds of volcanoes.

▲ The Andes are so tall that they are easily seen from space, as this satellite picture shows.

② Solve This

There are 5,280 feet (1,609 meters) in 1 mile. Which of the peaks is closest to being exactly 4 miles tall?

MATH ☑ POINT

Could you solve this problem if you used meters instead of feet?

PEAK	COUNTRY	HEIGHT
Aconcagua	Argentina	22,835 feet (6,960 meters)
Bonete	Argentina	22,175 feet (6,759 meters)
Ancohuma	Bolivia	21,085 feet (6,427 meters)
Illampu	Bolivia	20,892 feet (6,368 meters)
Cotopaxi	Ecuador	19,344 feet (5,896 meters)

Highlands

The **highlands** (HY-landz) are another major land feature. The Brazilian Highlands are near the east coast. The Guiana (gee-AH-nuh) Highlands are in the north. Both areas have very high **elevations** (eh-leh-VAY-shunz). Elevation is the distance above sea level.

Patagonia

Patagonia (pa-tuh-GOH-nee-uh) is found near the bottom tip of South America. It is a cold, barren place. Few things can survive there.

IT'S A FACT

Lake Titicaca lies on an Andes plain. With an elevation of 12,500 feet (3,810 meters), it is the world's highest lake that is navigable by ships. It is South America's second-largest lake after Lake Maracaibo.

◀ Lake Titicaca is the highest lake in the world that is navigable by large ships.

7

The Amazon Basin

The Amazon River is about 4,000 miles (6,436 kilometers) long. It is the world's second-longest river. The Amazon flows from west to east. It flows through a low region. This area is the Amazon **basin** (BAY-sin).

The Amazon has more water than any other river.

Many streams run down from the Andes Mountains. These streams join to form nearly 1,000 **tributaries** (TRIH-byuh-tair-eez). These waterways feed the great river.

Historical Perspective

Explorers have charted some parts of the Amazon basin, but much of this region is unmapped even today. People still explore the area. Some of them still get lost, just as explorers did long ago.

VENEZUELA
SURINAME
GUYANA
FRENCH GUIANA
COLOMBIA
EQUATOR
ECUADOR
Japurá R.
Negro R.
Putumayo R. **AMAZON**
BASIN Amazon R.
Marañón R.
Tapajós R.
Juruá R.
Purus R. Madeira R.
Xingú R.
Ucayali R.
BRAZIL
N
PERU
W   E
BOLIVIA
S

The Amazon **delta** (DEL-tuh) is about 165 miles (266 kilometers) wide at its widest point. A delta is a place where a river flows into an ocean, sea, or lake. Most deltas look like triangles.

Other Major Rivers

South America has three other big river basins. The Plata, the Orinoco, and the São Francisco all drain into the Atlantic Ocean.

Eyewitness Account

Former U.S. president Theodore Roosevelt explored the Amazon basin in 1914. He was amazed by the region's rugged beauty. Here is what he wrote at the start of the trip: *"No white man, had ever gone down or up this river, or seen the country through which we were passing. . . . The lofty and matted forest rose like a green wall on either hand. The trees were stately and beautiful, the looped and twisted vines hung from them like great ropes."*

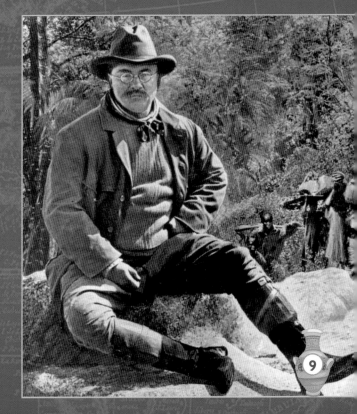

9

The Plains

The Pampas are plains in the southeast. This grassy region is about 750 miles (1,207 kilometers) wide. The Pampas have rich soil. Just enough rain falls there. This makes the Pampas good for farming.

A smaller plain lies in the north. This area is called the Llanos. The Llanos has rainy seasons and dry seasons.

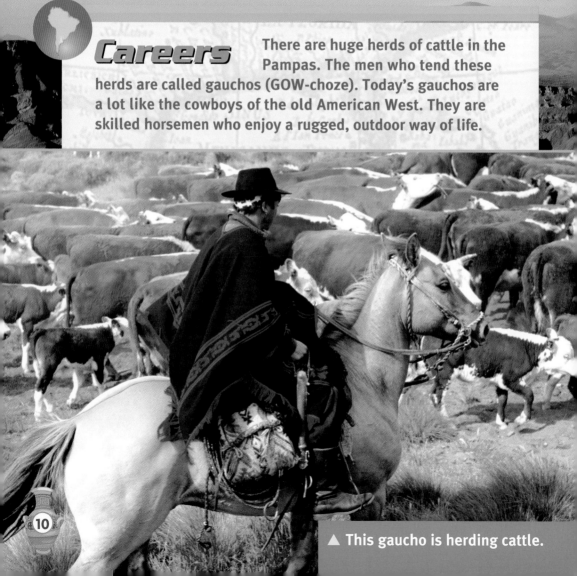

Careers

There are huge herds of cattle in the Pampas. The men who tend these herds are called gauchos (GOW-choze). Today's gauchos are a lot like the cowboys of the old American West. They are skilled horsemen who enjoy a rugged, outdoor way of life.

▲ This gaucho is herding cattle.

The Atacama Desert

The Atacama Desert is also dry. This cold desert is roughly 600 miles (965 kilometers) long and 100 miles (160 kilometers) wide. The desert is halfway down the west coast. Sand, salt, and **minerals** (MIH-nuh-rulz) cover the land.

Mountains block rain from falling in the desert. As a result, the Atacama is the driest place in the world. Less than 0.008 inches (0.2 millimeters) of rain falls there per year. Some parts have not had rain for more than forty years.

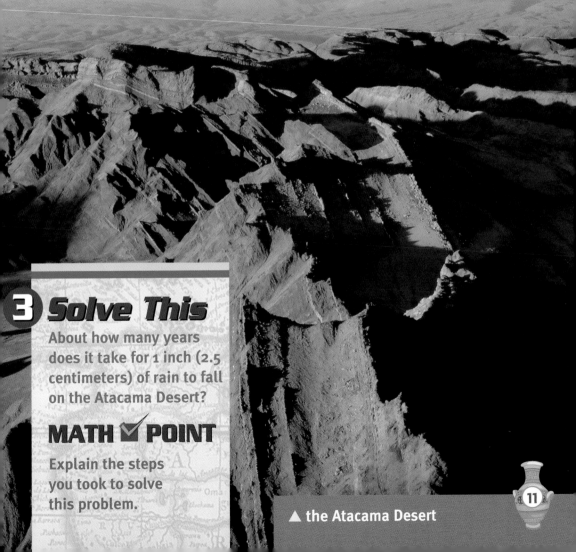

3 Solve This

About how many years does it take for 1 inch (2.5 centimeters) of rain to fall on the Atacama Desert?

MATH ☑ POINT

Explain the steps you took to solve this problem.

▲ the Atacama Desert

Human Geography of South America

South America has twelve countries and French Guiana. This small region is owned by France. Look at the map below. You can see where all twelve countries are.

One Continent, Many Cultures

People from many cultures live in South America. People celebrate different holidays. They have different ways of life. They also speak different languages.

They Made a Difference

In 1493, Pope Alexander VI drew a line on a map of the New World. He gave lands west of the line to Spain. He gave lands east of the line to Portugal. All of South America fell west of the line. The Spanish were delighted with this situation, but the Portuguese were unhappy. The two countries talked it over and agreed to move the line to the west. This change gave part of the continent's east coast to Portugal.

South America

- ○ National capital
- • City
- — International border

Geography is one reason for the differences. Long ago, early people were drawn to a few nice regions. These regions were far apart. People stayed where they settled. They felt no need to cross mountains and other **natural barriers** (NA-chuh-rul BAIR-ee-erz). As a result, groups did not have much contact with one another.

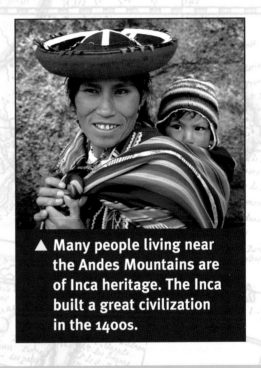

▲ Many people living near the Andes Mountains are of Inca heritage. The Inca built a great civilization in the 1400s.

4 Solve This Use the pie chart to answer the questions.

a. How many times could Ecuador fit into Peru?

b. Colombia, Venezuela, and Chile together equal the area of which single country?

c. Brazil and Argentina together make up what percentage of South America?

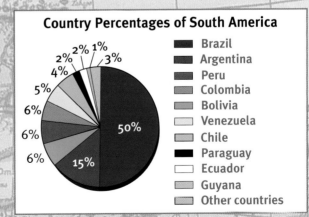

Country Percentages of South America

- Brazil
- Argentina
- Peru
- Colombia
- Bolivia
- Venezuela
- Chile
- Paraguay
- Ecuador
- Guyana
- Other countries

2% 2% 1%
2%
4%
5%
6%
6%
6%
50%
15%
3%

MATH ✓ POINT

Do your answers look reasonable?

13

Major Cities

Many South Americans live in big cities. The largest city is São Paulo (SOW POW-loh), Brazil. About 19 million people live there. Buenos Aires (BWAY-nus A-reez) is in Argentina. About 16.6 million people live there. Rio de Janeiro (REE-oh DAY zhuh-NAIR-oh), Brazil, has 11.2 million people. Lima (LEE-muh), Peru, has 7.5 million. More than thirty South American cities have populations over one million.

5 Solve This

Population density means the number of people in a given area. Look at the table below. Which country has the highest population density (most people per square mile)?

Country	Population in Millions	Area in Millions of Square Miles
Brazil	184.0	3.29 (8.52 sq. km)
Colombia	46.0	0.44 (1.14 sq. km)
Argentina	38.6	1.07 (2.77 sq. km)
Peru	27.9	0.50 (1.29 sq. km)
Venezuela	26.7	0.35 (0.91 sq. km)
Chile	16.1	0.29 (0.75 sq. km)

MATH ✓ POINT What information from the chart helped you answer this question?

City Locations

Geography makes travel hard in South America. As a result, most people settled in places that are easy to reach. Most of the large cities are near water. A few big towns are inland. These places have natural riches. For instance, Bogotá, Colombia, is east of the Andes. It is near good farmland. The same is true for Córdoba, Argentina. Córdoba is a mountain city with a **population** (pah-pyuh-LAY-shun) of 1.3 million people.

Santiago, Chile, has a population of more than four million. ▶

IT'S A FACT

The capital of Brazil is called Brasília. This inland city is not near any major natural resources. A natural resource is something found in nature that brings wealth to a country. Oil, gold, and lumber are all natural resources. Brasília is a planned city that was built between 1956 and 1960.

South America's cities are crowded. **Rural** (RER-ul) areas are not crowded. These places have room to spread out. Country people live and work there as they always have.

Life in the Andes

Long ago, people farmed and raised livestock in the Andes. Today, farmers still live there. They plant crops on flat strips in the hillsides. They may raise sheep and alpacas. They may raise llamas as well. Some people work in mines. They dig out gold, copper, lead, and other minerals.

Life in the Amazon Basin

About fifty native tribes still live in the Amazon basin. The tribes have very little to do with the modern world. They fish and hunt for meat. They grow or find their own fruits and vegetables.

▲ the Cuernos del Paine (Horns of Pain) Mountains in the Andes

Careers

A cultural anthropologist (an-thruh-PAH-luh-jist) is a scientist who studies the way people live. Some cultural anthropologists study modern people. Others are more interested in ancient ways of life. To study an Amazon tribe, a cultural anthropologist might live with the tribe for a long time. He or she would try to learn all about the speech, beliefs, and lifestyle of the group.

Life in Other Areas

The Pampas and Patagonia regions are large and empty. Cowboys tend herds of cattle in the Pampas. Farmers, shepherds, and miners scrape out a living in harsh, cold Patagonia.

▲ a sheepherder in Ecuador

 # Historical Perspective

In the early 1500s, millions of Indians lived in the Amazon basin. Most of these people were killed or died from disease when Spain ruled South America. No one knows for sure how many Indians are left. Experts think there are at least fifty-three tribes in Brazil and more in other countries. Together, all of South America's native tribes may contain 100,000 to 300,000 people.

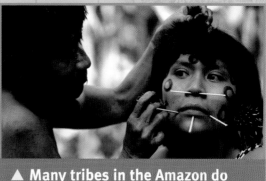

▲ Many tribes in the Amazon do not interact with the modern world. They practice their traditional cultures.

17

Moving to the Cities

South America's population patterns have changed in the past 100 years. In the early 1900s, rural people started to move to cities. Today, about three-fourths of people live in towns. About one-third of the population lives in the forty biggest cities.

✔ POINT

Make Connections

Do you live in a rural or urban area? What are the advantages of living where you do? What are the disadvantages?

▲ a crowded sidewalk in São Paulo, Brazil

Life in **urban** (ER-bun) areas seems easier than country life. The land and climate can make it hard to transport goods. People often think city jobs will make their lives simpler. But rural people cannot always get jobs in the cities. With no jobs or money, they cannot buy food. In spite of this, people stay in cities. They rarely return to the country way of life.

South America is called the "hollow continent." It got this name because so few people live inland. As more rural people head to big cities, the inland towns will get even emptier.

6 Solve This

In 2005, 21 babies were born for every 1,000 people in South America. In the same year, 6 people out of every 1,000 died. How many people were born for every one person who died?

MATH ☑ POINT

Is it possible to express your answer as a ratio?

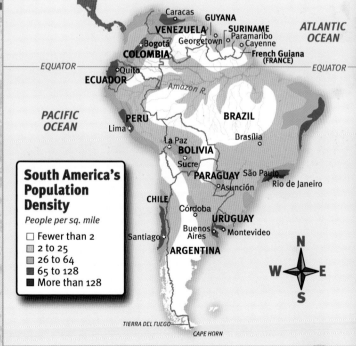

Caracas
GUYANA
VENEZUELA
SURINAME
Paramaribo
ATLANTIC
OCEAN
Georgetown
Cayenne
Bogotá
COLOMBIA
French Guiana
(FRANCE)
EQUATOR
Quito
ECUADOR
Amazon R.
EQUATOR
PACIFIC
OCEAN
PERU
BRAZIL
Lima
La Paz
Brasília
BOLIVIA
Sucre
PARAGUAY São Paulo
Asunción
Rio de Janeiro
CHILE
Córdoba
URUGUAY
Santiago
Buenos
Aires
Montevideo
ARGENTINA

South America's Population Density

People per sq. mile

- ☐ Fewer than 2
- 2 to 25
- 26 to 64
- 65 to 128
- More than 128

N
W E
S

TIERRA DEL FUEGO
CAPE HORN

Geography and the Economy

South America is rich in natural resources. Some nations rely on mines or farms to drive their **economy** (ih-KAH-nuh-mee). Other nations use their woods or waterways.

Minerals

Oil and gas are two major products. The biggest oil fields are found in Venezuela. Argentina has the largest natural gas fields. Other nations also have gas fields.

South America has many minerals as well. Brazil and Venezuela have iron ore. Chile and Peru have large copper mines. Brazil is known for its diamonds. The continent also has many tin, lead, and zinc mines.

PRIMARY SOURCE

In the early 1500s, South America was almost unknown to Europeans. By the early 1600s, the continent had been well explored.

▲ map of South America, around 1606

Agriculture

South American farms grow many crops. Farmers grow corn, bananas, and sugarcane. They also grow coffee, cocoa, rubber, wheat, and cotton.

Ranchers raise large herds of cattle. Some ranchers raise llamas, alpacas, sheep, and goats, too.

Forests and Fishing

Wood products and seafood are common, too. Most trees come from the Amazon basin. Fisherman work off the coasts of Peru, Ecuador, and Argentina. People in Brazil, Ecuador, and Peru also raise shrimp on farms in the ocean.

7 Solve This

In 2004, each ton of Argentinean beef sold for $2,203. One ton equals 2,000 pounds. How much did each pound of beef cost?

MATH ☑ POINT

Could you solve this problem without knowing how many pounds are in a ton?

This map shows where ▶ the major industries and natural resources are located in South America.

Resources

- 🐄 Cocoa
- ☕ Coffee
- 🌽 Corn
- Cotton
- 🐟 Fishing
- Forest products
- 🍇 Fruits
- ⚑ Gas
- 🐂 Livestock
- ✕ Mining and minerals
- ⚒ Oil
- Rubber
- 🐑 Sheep
- Sugarcane
- Tropical fruits
- ⸸ Wheat

Trade Barriers

Long ago, very little trading went on inside South America. Traders could not travel across the mountains, rivers, and plains. The coast had few ports where ships could dock. It was hard to move goods around. So most resources stayed wherever they were.

IT'S A FACT

The Amazon is the second-longest river in the world, but it is number one in terms of water volume. The river dumps about 30 billion gallons (114 billion liters) of fresh water into the Atlantic Ocean each second. That's about 20 times the output of Niagara Falls! During rainy times, parts of the Amazon swell from 7 miles (11 kilometers) across to more than 25 miles (40 kilometers) wide.

people canoeing on the Amazon River in Brazil ▲

Trade Routes

It is still hard to travel from place to place in South America. But today, people are building more roads and railways. Tunnels run through parts of the Andes. A highway crosses the Amazon basin.

Cargo ships can sail up the Amazon and other main rivers. Airplanes carry things to remote areas. These changes make it easier to move goods.

▲ The Transamazonian Highway runs 3,400 miles (5,472 kilometers) through the thick Amazon Rain Forest.

Major Exports

South America sells many things to the rest of the world. Brazil **exports** (ek-SPORTS) more beef than any other country. Venezuela sells oil and gas. Colombia exports coffee. South American crops line the shelves in grocery stores around the world. By selling these things, countries earn money. This keeps their economies strong.

▲ Coffee is grown on large plantations in South America. It is an important export.

Used at Home

South America does not export all of its products. In Argentina, people eat beef from local herds. They eat more beef than any other people in the world! People in Peru and Chile eat the fish they catch. Wood from the Amazon basin is used to heat local homes. These products and others form the basis of local economies.

▲ gauchos driving cattle across the Pampas, a vast plain of south-central South America

8 Solve This

Countries earn money from agriculture (farms and ranches), industry (nonagricultural products), and services (labor that does not involve goods). Use the graph to answer these questions.

a. Which countries earn more money from agriculture than industry?

b. Which country earns about 68% of its money from services?

c. Agriculture makes up what percent of Brazil's economy?

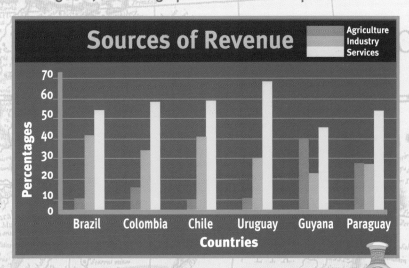

Sources of Revenue

Agriculture
Industry
Services

Percentages

Brazil Colombia Chile Uruguay Guyana Paraguay

Countries

Human Effects

As populations grow, more resources are needed. Some resources, like crops, can be replaced quickly. Others cannot. Oil, gas, and minerals are not renewable.

Human effects are greatest in the Amazon basin. People cut down huge stretches of rain forest to get wood. They are cutting down trees faster than new trees can grow. This is bad for the environment.

Rain forests are very important. More than fifty percent of all animal and plant species live in rain forests. And up to fifty percent of the world's oxygen is made by the Amazon Rain Forest. These are very important resources. They need to be protected.

▲ In Brazil, extensive areas of the Amazon Rain Forest have been destroyed by loggers and farmers.

Changing the Land

As people use up resources, they will look for more. They will move to more remote places.

People will build new roads, railways, and airports for easy access. These things will change South America's landscape.

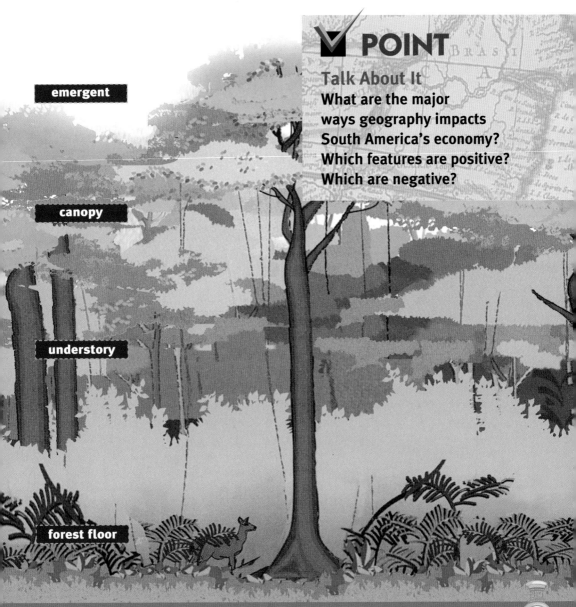

✔ POINT

Talk About It
What are the major ways geography impacts South America's economy? Which features are positive? Which are negative?

emergent

canopy

understory

forest floor

▲ **The Amazon Rain Forest has four distinct layers.**

Conclusion

To understand South America, you must study its geography. The continent's location affects the climate and landforms. Those features affect the people of South America. They affect history, culture, and trade.

Today, natural barriers that once kept people apart are less of a challenge. People have found or built ways over mountains and plains. They have carved paths through the rain forest. People use phones and computers to talk with one another over long distances.

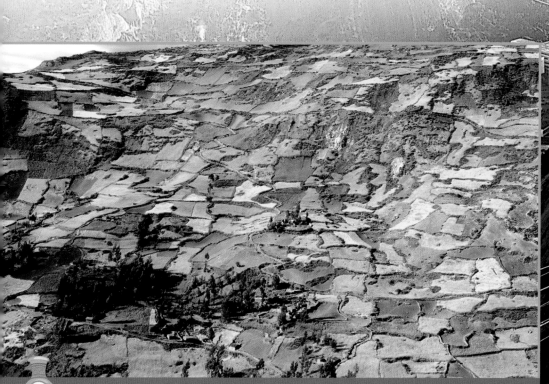

▲ Advances in communication have helped people in rural areas, like this region in Peru, keep in touch with others.

Cities in South America will keep growing. Its countries will try harder to work together. Still, some things may never change.

People will still celebrate their different ways of life. This land of extremes will keep growing and thriving.

▲ Rio de Janeiro, Brazil

1. Page 5
About 83 percent
The total length of South
America is about 4,700 miles.
4,700 – 800 = 3,900 miles.
This is the length south of the
equator. 3,900 ÷ 4,700 = 83%.
This is the percentage of the
length below the equator.
(The total length is 7,560 km.
7,560 km – 1,287 km = 6,273
km. This is the length south of
the equator. 6,273 ÷ 7,560 =
83%. This is the percentage
of length below the equator.)

2. Page 6
Mount Ancohuma
5,280 feet x 4 = 21,120 feet
(1,609 m x 4 = 6,436 m)
Mount Ancohuma's height
of 21,085 feet (6,427 m) is
closest to 21,120 (6,436).

3. Page 11
About 125 years
1 inch of rain ÷ the total rainfall
per year of 0.008 = 125 years.
(0.2 mm of rain per year = 0.02
cm. 2.5 cm of rain ÷ the total
rainfall per year of 0.02 cm =
125 years)

4. Page 13
a. Three times: (Ecuador = 2%;
Peru = 6%) 6 ÷ 2 = 3
b. Argentina: (Colombia =6%;
Venezuela = 5%; Chile = 4%)
6 + 5 + 4 = 15%; Argentina = 15%

c. 65 percent, or about two-
thirds: (Brazil = 50%; Argentina
= 15%) 50 + 15 = 65%

5. Page 14
Colombia has 104.55 people per
square mile (40.35 per sq. km),
more than any other country
on the list.
Divide each country's
population by its area to get
the number of people per
square mile (kilometer).

6. Page 19
3.5 people were born for every
one who died.
Divide the number of people
who were born by the number
who died. 21 ÷ 6 = 3.5.

7. Page 21
About $1.10
Divide the price per ton by the
number of pounds in one ton.
$2,203 ÷ 2,000 = $1.10 per
pound.

8. Page 25
a. Guyana and Paraguay
b. Uruguay
c. About 11%

basin	(BAY-sin) a shallow, bowl-shaped area of land drained by a river or stream (page 8)
continent	(KAHN-tih-nent) one of Earth's seven major land divisions (page 2)
delta	(DEL-tuh) a place where a river flows into an ocean, sea, or lake (page 9)
economy	(ih-KAH-nuh-mee) the way a nation manages its resources (page 20)
elevation	(eh-leh-VAY-shun) altitude; height in comparison to sea level (page 7)
equator	(ih-KWAY-ter) an imaginary line that separates Earth's Northern and Southern hemispheres (page 4)
export	(ek-SPORT) to send goods to another country to be sold (page 24)
geography	(jee-AH-gruh-fee) the study of Earth's features (page 2)
highland	(HY-land) high or mountainous region (page 7)
mineral	(MIH-nuh-rul) a chemical substance found in nature, such as oil and gas, metals, gems, and some rocks (page 11)
natural barrier	(NA-chuh-rul BAIR-ee-er) any land or water feature that blocks travel, trade, or other activities (page 13)
plain	(PLANE) a flat region with few or no trees (page 3)
population	(pah-pyuh-LAY-shun) the group of people living in a certain place (page 15)
rural	(RER-ul) having to do with the countryside (page 16)
settlement	(SEH-tul-ment) movement into a region for the purpose of living there (page 3)
trade	(TRADE) the purchase and sale of goods (page 3)
tributary	(TRIH-byuh-tair-ee) a stream that feeds larger streams, rivers, or lakes (page 8)
urban	(ER-bun) having to do with cities (page 19)

Index

Write in Your Social Studies Journal

Choose one of the following prompts to write about in your journal. Make drawings, charts, or other graphic features to help you organize your thoughts.

1. Write about the geographic area of South America that you find most interesting. What about this area interests you? Make a list of other things about the area you would like to know. (Make connections)

2. Review the text. Explain how life in rural areas is similar to and different from life in urban areas. (Compare and contrast)

3. The author included information about the effects of South America's growing population on its natural resources and its land. Why do you think the author included this information? How do you think she feels about this topic? Support your answers with evidence from the text. (Evaluate author's purpose and point of view)

redits
roject Editor: Vicki Rushworth
rt Director: Glenn Davis
irector of Photography: Lynn Shen
teracy Consultants: Tammy Jones and Katherine Scraper
oncepting and Editorial Services: Creative Media Applications

hoto Credits
over, Title Page, 7A, 7B, 10–12, 16, 17B, 28: Getty Images; Pages 2–3: Alison Wright/
orbis; Page 6: Corbis; Pages 7, 32: Pablo Corral V/Corbis; Page 10: Kit Houghton/
orbis; Page 15: Fridmar Damm/zefa/Corbis; Page 17A: Owen Franken/ Corbis; Page
3: Collart Herve/Corbis Sygma; Page 24: Enzo & Paolo Ragazzini/ Corbis; Page 25: Kit
oughton/Corbis; Page 26: Rickey Rogers/Reuters/Corbis

BRIDGES

BENCHMARK EDUCATION COMPANY
629 Fifth Avenue • Pelham, NY • 10803

Benchmark
EDUCATION

Geography of South America

Welcome to South America! This vast continent is home to towering mountains, huge lakes, immense rivers, and the largest rainforest in the world. Journey through South America's many regions and learn how its geography has shaped the lives of its people.

ABOUT THE AUTHOR

Kristine Hirschmann has written more than 120 books and countless activity kits for children. She holds a B.A. in Psychology from Dartmouth College. Kristine has visited Brazil, where she saw and enjoyed some of South America's many wonders.

ISBN 978-1-4509-2871-7

BENCHMARK EDUCATION COMPANY